DODD, MEAD WONDERS BOOKS include WONDERS OF:

CATTLE. Scuro
CORALS AND CORAL REEFS. Jacobson
  and Franz
CROWS. Blassingame
DONKEYS. Lavine and Scuro
DRAFT HORSES. Lavine and Casey
DUST. McFall
EAGLE WORLD. Lavine
EGRETS, BITTERNS, AND HERONS.
  Blassingame
ELEPHANTS. Lavine and Scuro
FLIGHTLESS BIRDS. Lavine
FROGS AND TOADS. Blassingame
GEESE AND SWANS. Fegely
GOATS. Lavine and Scuro
HIPPOS. Lavine
LIONS. Schaller
MARSUPIALS. Lavine
MICE. Lavine
MULES. Lavine and Scuro

PEACOCKS. Lavine
PIGS. Lavine and Scuro
PONIES. Lavine and Casey
RACCOONS. Blassingame
RATTLESNAKES. Chace
RHINOS. Lavine
SEA HORSES. Brown
SEALS AND SEA LIONS. Brown
SHEEP. Lavine and Scuro
SNAILS AND SLUGS. Jacobson and
  Franz
SPONGES. Jacobson and Pang
TURKEYS. Lavine and Scuro
TURTLE WORLD. Blassingame
WILD DUCKS. Fegely
WOODCHUCKS. Lavine
WORLD OF BEARS. Bailey
WORLD OF HORSES. Lavine and Casey
ZEBRAS. Scuro

WONDERS OF TURKEYS

Sigmund A. Lavine & Vincent Scuro
Illustrated with photographs and old prints

DODD, MEAD & COMPANY New York

For Caspar, who deserves it

ILLUSTRATIONS COURTESY OF: Food and Agriculture Organization of the United Nations, 20, 31, 32; Sigmund A. Lavine's collection, photographed by Nickolas J. Krach, 10, 22, 24; Minnesota Turkey Growers Association, courtesy of National Turkey Federation, Reston, Virginia, *frontispiece*, 34, 43, 46, 48 *bottom*, 49, 50 *top*; National Turkey Federation, Reston, Virginia, 13, 38, 40, 47, 57, 58, 59; National Archives, 26, 27, 28, 37, 61; Nicholas Turkey Breeding Farms, courtesy of National Turkey Federation, 36, 48 *top*, 50 *bottom*; USDA Photo, 6, 19, 52; USDA Photo by Murray Berman, 17; USDA Photo by Marianne Pernold, 55; Victoria and Albert Museum, London, 21.

NOTE: According to experts, it is difficult to identify turkey pictures as to breed, because of the amount of crossbreeding that has been done.

For more information on the American wild turkey, its conservation and wise management, contact the National Wild Turkey Federation, P.O. Box 530, Edgefield, SC, 29824-0530, 803-637-3106. The NWTF sponsors an educationally oriented program for young people up to age 17 entitled JAKES, Juniors Acquiring Knowledge, Ethics and Sportsmanship. Members receive a quarterly newsletter, *Pinfeathers*.

1 2 3 4 5 6 7 8 9 10

Library of Congress Cataloging in Publication Data

Lavine, Sigmund A.
  Wonders of turkeys.

  Includes index.
  Summary: Describes the evolution, physical characteristics, and behavior of wild and domestic turkeys and discusses the various breeds and their role in American tradition and folklore.
  1. Wild turkeys—Juvenile literature. 2. Turkeys—Juvenile literature. [1. Turkeys. 2. Wild turkeys]
I. Scuro, Vincent. II. Title.
QL696.G254L38 1984   598'.619   84-1638
ISBN 0-396-08333-1

Fr___iece: A Broad Breasted Large White turkey

CONTENTS

1 Meet the Turkey   7

2 Lore of the Turkey   12

3 Wild Turkeys   25

4 Domesticated Turkeys   30
   A Flock of Turkeys   37

5 The Turkey Industry   45

6 A Very Valuable Bird   53

7 Turkey Shooting   60

   Index   63

These turkeys look to be the very spirit of Thanksgiving.

One

MEET THE TURKEY

The turkey is misnamed!

Its common name implies that it originated in Turkey. This is not true. Neither the wild turkey (*Meleagris gallopavo*) of North America, the ocellated turkey (*Agriocharis ocellata*) of Central America, nor their domesticated relatives have any ties to present-day Turkey or the Turkish Empire of yesteryear. The turkey is a native of the New World.

There are numerous explanations of the origin of the word turkey. Some ornithologists—students of bird life—maintain that turkey was derived from *firkee*, an American Indian name for the bird. Other experts claim that the turkey's call, *turc, turc, turc*, is the source of the common name. Still other naturalists point out that shortly after the turkey was introduced into Europe in the early sixteenth century it was confused with a species of guinea fowl highly prized by cooks in the service of nobles and wealthy individuals. Despite the fact that the guinea fowl came from Africa, it was generally assumed that it originated in Turkey.

Right to left: wild turkey, domestic turkey, and three guinea fowl, topped by a blue peacock

In 1552, Sir Thomas Elyot described "birdes which we doo call hennes of Genny or Turkie Henne." Some early naturalists suggested that Elyot's "birdes" were called turkeys because of the supposed resemblance between the red adornments on the bird's head and the fez, a red, tasseled felt cap formerly worn as a national headdress by Turkish men. This explanation is perhaps the most fanciful of all the attempts to trace the source of the word.

Actually, it is logical to assume the bird gots its common name as the result of the mistaken idea that it was a native of Turkey. As a matter of fact, this conviction persisted throughout Europe long after it had been established that the turkey was a native of the New World. For example, in 1755, when Dr. Samuel Johnson published his famous *Dictionary of the English Language*, he defined turkey as "A large domestick fowl brought from Turkey."

Eventually, no one confused guinea fowl from Africa with the turkey. But by the time the distinction was clear to naturalists and laymen alike, turkey had become the accepted name for the bird imported from the New World—and it still is. Incidentally, the turkey is the only race of poultry that originated in the Western Hemisphere.

It is interesting to note that long before the turkey was known in Europe, the word was in widespread use throughout the British Isles. An early chronicler recorded that, during the reign of Edward III (1312–1377), one William Yoo had royal permission to emblazon "Three Turkey-cocks in their pride proper" on his coat of arms. As no turkeys had as yet been imported into England from the Americas, the birds displayed by Yoo were undoubtedly peacocks.

Scientists have placed turkeys in the Order Galliformes (chicken-like birds), which includes domestic fowl, pheasants, partridges, grouse, and quail.

Ornithologists are agreed that turkeys have inhabited much of North and Central America for at least ten million years. Proof of this is furnished by fossils that have been unearthed in places as far apart as New Jersey and California. While most of these remains are of birds indistinguishable from living turkeys, more than seven hundred specimens of an extinct species have been found in Los Angeles' famous Rancho La Brea tar pits.

The scientist who originally studied the bones discovered at La Brea described them as those of a fossil peacock of Asiatic origin. However, further research revealed that they were the bones of a turkey. This bird was given the scientific name *Parapavo californicus* (peacock-like bird from California). Restorations of *californicus* by paleontologists—experts on fossil

This 100-year-old picture of the ocellated turkey wrongly identified the bird as belonging to the same genus as the domestic and wild turkeys of North America. However, this handsome resident of Central America has been placed by modern zoologists in a new genus because of its physical characteristics and has been given the scientific designation Agriocharis ocellata. Note how the protuberance above the nose has extended and dropped down on the near bird.

remains—indicate that it bore a closer resemblance to the ocellated turkey than to the wild turkeys of North America.

As indicated, the turkey unquestionably originated in the Americas. Yet, although there is no evidence that it ever lived elsewhere, certain authorities claim the turkey ". . . may have evolved from an early dispersal of pheasant relatives to America from Asia." Indeed, formerly, the wild turkey was not only thought to have an Old World ancestry but also was considered so similar to the pheasant that it was placed in the same family.

In order to determine the true relationship between turkeys and pheasants, scientists have undertaken complicated experiments in crossbreeding. Meanwhile, authorities continue to debate whether or not the turkey should be reclassified and placed with the pheasants or kept in a separate family. Some of the arguments advanced in this dispute deal with anatomical and physiological details far too complex for laymen to follow. On the other hand, some of the reasons offered for considering the turkeys a separate family from the pheasants are easily understood by non-experts. They deal with differences in muscles, head furnishings, and plumage.

Two

Lore of the Turkey

Turkey meat from wild or domesticated birds was a staple in the diet of many Indian tribes. However, the Cheyennes would not eat turkey for fear it might make them cowardly. This belief probably stemmed from the wild turkey's habit of running away as fast as possible when threatened. The Papago and Apache also considered the turkey timid and, as a result, neither ate its flesh nor used the bird's feathers on arrows.

While other tribes might feed freely on turkey, taboos controlled how it was cooked. Certain procedures had to be followed in order to insure that various deities would not be provoked. Meanwhile, in pueblos scattered through the region now known as the states of Arizona and New Mexico, the turkey was held to be sacred. It was not eaten even in times of famine. Actually, most Southwest tribes employed the turkey in their religious ceremonies. As it was in Mexico, the turkey was held to be a sacrificial bird. Skeletons of turkeys with the head missing have been found in the graves of primitive tribesmen containing offerings to the dead, with corn provided for the birds.

Drawing depicts a wild turkey.

This old print shows the reliance of some Indians on the use of feathers for decoration.

In Arizona, archaeologists—antiquities experts—have discovered burial sites where turkeys were interred with humans.

It would take a book several times the size of this one to detail how the Indians of the Southwest used turkey feathers in religious ceremonies. Not only were these feathers vital to the ritual manufacture of prayer sticks, masks, and headdresses but also they were employed by both priests and laymen as they conducted various rites.

Early anthropologists—specialists in the science of man— noted that the turkeys kept by the Hopi had "a ragged aspect." Investigation revealed that the birds were frequently plucked by their owners in the belief that turkey feathers had the power to bring rain. The feathers also were thought to provide protection. This is why the Indians of Texas stuck turkey feathers

14

in anthills as they trekked through the countryside.

Both the Zuni and the Navajo feature the turkey in their accounts of how humans reached the Earth. These legends also explain the turkey's tail-feather markings. According to the Navajo, their ancient ancestors were in danger of being engulfed by a raging flood when they lived in the Third World, a wide and beautiful land like the Earth. To escape drowning, men and women, aided by all the animals, piled the mountains that mark the Four Directions on top of one another. When this was done, a reed was planted on the top of the massive pile.

Within a very short time, the reed grew so high that it pierced the sky, and humans and animals entered it through an opening just above the root. Because Turkey was the last in line, he was given the task of warning everyone when to start climbing up the inside of the reed. It was decided that he should sound the alarm when the rising waters wet his feet and tail feathers. This soon happened, Turkey cried out, and the people and animals began climbing. Eventually, they reached the sky and entered the Fourth World. But circumstances forced them to migrate once more until they arrived in the world in which the Navajo now live.

Navajo tradition maintains that great changes have taken place in the tribe's way of life since their ancestors climbed to the Fourth World. However, one thing is the same—the turkey's tail feathers are still light colored from being soaked by the flood.

While the Indians of the Southwest revered the turkey, northern tribes had mixed emotions about the bird. Some tribes were convinced that it was a friend of man and battled evil spirits. Others credited the turkey with showing humans how to plant corn and tobacco. Still others maintained that sorcerers turned themselves into turkeys so that they could approach those they wished to bewitch.

Tribes that were sure the turkey had great powers often duplicated the bird's motions during various ceremonies. In their courtship dance, Huichol braves mimicked a gobbler courting hens. During the Ute *tho'nka-ni-tcap*, both men and women thrust the head forward, wagged it from side to side, and heeled and toed erratically. Comanche, Choctaw, Delaware, and Seminole dancers also imitated turkeys. Both Sioux and Chickasaw women, who were sure the turkey caused illness, tried to propitiate the bird in a special dance.

No one knows how long the Indians have copied the strutting and preening of the tom turkey. But we do know that the "Turkey Trot" was a most popular ballroom dance in the early years of this century. It was not graceful—the dancers circled the floor in short, jerky steps.

Not only the Indians associated the turkey with evil. In Ireland, witches supposedly had the power to turn themselves into gobblers. Irish folklore also contains many tales of ghosts that take the form of a turkey. On the other side of the world, the Tagalogs of the Philippines fear Patiank, a malicious blood-sucking being who often is disguised as a turkey.

One of the most unusual beliefs about the turkey maintains that the bird can make warts disappear. One way is quite simple—merely rub a wart with a kernel of corn and feed the kernel to a turkey. The second method is far more complicated. First, using a white turkey feather, grease must be removed from the wheel of a wagon drawn by a white mule. Then, if the greased feather is rubbed on the wart for three days at 3:30 P.M. sharp, the wart will fall off.

Superstitious individuals also hold that it is bad luck to count

16

The superstitious believe that it is bad luck to count a flock of turkeys. They say that a white turkey feather rubbed in the grease of a wheel on a wagon drawn by a white mule will help remove warts.

a flock of turkeys, believing that, if they are counted, the birds will die. Perhaps the most widespread superstition featuring the turkey is based on the relationship of the ancient foes, fox and poultry. In both the United States and Europe, there are those who claim that a fox, by rolling over and over, can charm high-roosting turkeys to fly to the ground.

According to the Aztecs, who ritually strangled turkeys in sacrifice to their gods, it was a sure sign of rain if live turkeys took a dust bath. Today, New England farmers claim the birds are forecasting a storm if they stand with their backs to the wind. Rural residents of the Middle West maintain that if turkeys perch on the top of a building, it is a warning of cold weather. It is also widely believed that if turkeys gobble, preen, and then ruffle their feathers, it will storm.

Common speech has not overlooked the turkey. The bird's characteristics have inspired numerous idiomatic sayings. An individual whose face becomes flushed with anger is said to turn "red as a turkey cock." This is a reference to the brilliance of the head and neck furnishings of courting males. The tom's dignified walk is the source of the saying "He struts like a turkey cock."

"To be as proud as a lame turkey" stems from the gobbler's grand manner. While "She's as shy as a wild turkey" is self-explanatory, there seems no logical reason why those associated with the theater call a show that fails to draw audiences a turkey.

Anyone who is "sneaking as a turkey gobbler ketch'd out in the rain" is not to be trusted. The Yankee "He is driving turkeys to market" is a polite way of saying someone is too drunk to walk straight. This expression is based on the experiences of the men who rounded up vast herds of turkeys and drove them to towns. Turkey drives never went in a straight line—the birds wandered far and wide, despite the efforts of the herders to keep them moving straight ahead.

Without a doubt, the best-known idiomatic expression featuring the turkey is "Let's talk turkey." It means to avoid fancy words and speak plainly and directly. Conversations of this type are apt to take considerable energy, and it is very possible that those that take part in them become "hungry as the chap who said a turkey was too much for one and not enough for two."

18

Easily frightened and stampeded, domestic turkeys are moved gently down a slope, urged on by burlap bags. It is difficult to drive turkeys in a straight line.

Nothing is "poorer than a turkey in summer" unless it is "Job's turkey that was so poorly it had to lean against the fence to stand up." Both these sayings are employed when describing a horse or cow not in good condition.

Not too long ago, "turkey" was the cant term for a fifty-cent piece. While this example of American slang is no longer in use, most residents of the United States know that "Turkey Day" is a popular synonym for Thanksgiving. The special jargons of tramps and loggers also make use of the word. Tramps call the canvas bag in which they carry their few possessions a turkey, while loggers employ this term to identify a bedroll. Meanwhile, wherever pure white zinc ore is mined, the more common, bright-yellow zinc ore is known as "turkey fat" ore.

The turkey has not only made popular speech more colorful but also the bird has given its name to numerous physical features of the North American continent. Captain John Smith,

19

leader of the Virginia colony, was the first to name a particular place after the turkey—Turkey Isle in the James River. Later mapmakers copied Smith and, whenever they encountered an abundance of turkeys, named a body of water or a land formation after the birds. However, Mount Tom in western Massachusetts was named for a different reason. It is a memorial to the state's last native wild turkey gobbler, which died over a century ago.

When Cortez received Montezuma's ambassadors during the Spanish invasion of Mexico in 1519, the men presented the leader of the conquistadors with six gold turkeys. The description of these beautiful statuettes in the chronicle of Cortez' expedition is the first mention of the turkey in art. However, long before the Spanish ravaged Mexico, the turkey was inspiring artists.

The craftsmen who produced early representations of turkeys are unknown Indians. These skilled artisans fashioned terra cotta jugs with handles formed in the shape of a turkey's head

Turkeys thrive in Mexico today, as they did in the time of the conquistadors.

This gobbler was painted for Jahangir, Emperor of Hindustan, by the Mogul artist Ustad Mansur in 1621. The bird was imported from the Portuguese colony at Goa on the southwest coast of India.

and neck, painted turkeys on bowls, and sketched the bird on the walls of *estufas* (underground chambers in which religious ceremonies were held). Both wild and domesticated turkeys were delineated by Indian artists.

A wild turkey was the subject of the first European illustration of a turkey. It appeared in Konrad Gesner's *Historia Animalium*, which was published in 1555. Since Gesner's work appeared, the list of etchers, engravers, painters, and sculptors who have portrayed the wild turkey has grown tremendously. Such a list would include, among others, Peter Bruegel, Simon de Vlieger, Titian Peale, Louis Agassiz Fuertes, Lynn Bogue Hunt, and Roger Tory Peterson. But the best-known repre-

21

Old print from an article about American game birds, published in 1865, resembles Audubon's famous picture, although it bears different initials.

sentations of wild turkeys are those painted by John J. Audubon for his monumental *The Birds of America.*

Artists have also depicted the domestic turkey. Among them are the Venetian Jacopo Bassano, Sir Nathaniel Bacon of England, and the Flemish master, Melchior d' Hondecoeter.

For centuries, craftsmen have fashioned turkeys from clay,

22

metal, and wood. Queen Elizabeth I had a saltcellar shaped like a gobbler. It was carved in agate and decorated with gold and precious stones. In the late nineteenth century, Giovanni da Bologna cast a turkey in bronze. Two modern American sculptors have created turkeys in stainless steel.

A turkey decorated one of the plates used by President Rutherford Hayes at the White House. Today, turkey plates are commonplace—but decorating tableware with turkeys is nothing new. It has been done in both Europe and the New World for three hundred years.

In the days of slavery, the turkey was mentioned in work songs. But none of these compositions was as popular as "Turkey in the Straw." This rollicking tune has delighted generations of Americans.

Actually, the turkey is far more prominent in literature than in music. It struts through the works of Francis Beaumont, John Fletcher, William Hazlitt, and Shakespeare. The bird has also inspired dozens of poets, including Marjorie Fleming, Ogden Nash, and Richard Wilbur. While the majority of poems about the turkey are concerned with Thanksgiving, Oliver Wendell Holmes ignores that holiday. He asks: If it is true that when in Rome one should do as the Romans do, wouldn't it be proper to gobble when in Turkey?

No bit of American folklore is so firmly established as the belief that Thanksgiving Day has been celebrated annually ever since the Pilgrims held the first feast in 1621. This is untrue. It was not until 1863, that President Abraham Lincoln—at the urging of Sarah Josepha Hale, editor of *Godey's Lady's Book*—set aside the last Thursday in November "as a day for national thanksgiving, praise and prayer."

An old postcard depicting favorite birds of the United States

In 1939, President Franklin D. Roosevelt moved the date chosen by Lincoln forward one week to have more time between Thanksgiving and Christmas. Roosevelt's action was supported by businessmen because it lengthened the holiday shopping season. But other groups resented tampering with tradition. This led to confusion as to when Thanksgiving should be celebrated. Eventually, the change was accepted by most Americans.

Three

WILD TURKEYS

America's wild turkeys inhabit forests and brush lands from New England as far north as the Dakotas, and from southern Ontario to southern Mexico. However, the three Pacific Coast contiguous states have never had a native wild turkey population. Neither have Idaho, Montana, Nevada, and Wyoming.

The characteristics of the wild turkey enable it to survive the dangers of America's untamed regions. Nature has endowed these birds with excellent hearing, making it extremely difficult for any creature to approach without being detected. A wild turkey's eyesight is exceptionally keen, six times more powerful than a human's. High-flying birds that are mere specks to a man without binoculars can easily be seen by a wild turkey. Since turkeys see in color and have a 300-degree view of the world, they can detect the movement of even a heavily camouflaged intruder. However, a turkey's night vision and depth perception are poor.

Wild turkeys also have a poor sense of smell but their sense of taste is keen. They love to eat berries, grass, and insects.

Wild turkeys have excellent hearing and keen eyesight.

Their favorite food is acorns. These birds "chew" the nuts they pick off the ground, softening them with acids in the crop (a pouch in the gullet where food is prepared for digestion), then passing the nuts into the gizzard. Here the hulls are pulverized. Wild turkeys prefer to dine at dawn. Some observers say they are notorious nibblers, tasting a bit of one food, then part of another, then still another. It has been noted that a wild turkey's appetite decreases during the mating season which occurs in the spring.

Among the males, most of the mating is done by dominant toms. A "pecking order" is determined through fierce fighting, which occasionally results in the death of one of the combatants. The strongest gobblers earn the right to mate.

26

The courtship ritual of the wild tom consists of a showy display designed to attract the females. First, he spreads out his upper plumage and tail feathers; then he struts about, gobbling to the hens. He mates with several different females during the season.

Hens make their nests of dried leaves in concealed locations on the ground. Here, nine to twenty creamy-white eggs with red-brown speckles are laid in a clutch. The eggs hatch after twenty-eight days of incubation. Incidentally, more than one hen may share the same nest, which accounts for the dozens of eggs found in some places.

All turkeys are born with the instinct for flying. One newly hatched discovers how to fly about two weeks after it is born. It practices until it feels confident about leaving the ground. With time, speed develops. An adult turkey can fly thirty to thirty-five miles per hour for long distances and fifty-five miles

A battle between two wild turkey gobblers during mating season at the Wichita Mountains National Wildlife Refuge, Oklahoma

ABOVE: *A wild turkey nest in the oak brush of Kerr County, Texas*

BELOW: *Eastern wild turkey in the Ozark region, Missouri*

per hour in short spurts. Compared to most other birds, turkeys are not considered to be fast flyers, nor do they fly very high.

Although they are not the fleetest birds on foot, wild turkeys are good runners. Their strides, which are about four feet in length, enable them to achieve speeds up to twenty-five miles per hour. Males are famous for their full-striding run with heads thrown back and wings dragging on the ground. Some observers think these birds prefer running to flying.

Sometimes turkeys are very noisy. Wild toms love to gobble when they hear loud sounds. They also gobble when they settle in for the night. The wing flapping of a wild turkey landing in its roost is so loud it can be heard for miles.

Are wild turkeys "chicken," as some Indian tribes believed? Few people will say that these are brave birds—they have been known to run for cover at the first sight of a golden eagle. Yet, for some unknown reason, wild turkeys remain calm when a buzzard or a hawk circles their area. It is not clear whether this response is due to indifference or lack of fear.

Before human expansion destroyed much of the wild turkey's habitat, the birds were abundant throughout their ranges. Flocks numbering thousands of birds were commonplace. Market hunters often shot several hundred a day, selling them for six cents apiece! Today, state game commissions strictly regulate wild turkey hunting, thus preserving these native birds for future generations to enjoy.

Four

DOMESTICATED TURKEYS

The scribes who accompanied the conquistadors seeking the fabulous Cities of Gold in the Old Southwest have left detailed accounts of how the natives domesticated the turkey. These records not only tell how the bird was raised and bred but also describe how important a part it played in Aztec life. Besides being a staple food, the turkey was considered a suitable article of tribute. Thus, the Emperor Montezuma received some 365,000 turkeys every year from his subjects. Many of these were fed to the meat-eaters in Montezuma's zoo.

Both Francisco Fernandez, who explored the northern coast of Yucatan in 1517, and Hernando Cortez, who conquered Mexico in 1519, took turkeys with them when they returned to Spain. Meanwhile, Antonio Espejo, Francisco Coronado, Augustin Rodriguez, and the other adventurers who sought gold and glory in other areas of Mexico and Central America frequently dined on turkey when visiting pueblos. These explorers also shipped turkeys to Spain and, by the time they returned home, the bird was common not only in Spain but also in the barnyards of England, France, and Italy.

Although turkeys originated in the Western Hemisphere, they have been distributed to other parts of the world. A turkey farm in the Serres Valley, Greece.

Among the livestock English settlers carried to the New World were descendants of the turkeys that had been introduced into England in 1524. These were small birds, not nearly as attractive or tasty as the big, handsome, eastern wild turkeys that lived in hardwood forests along the Atlantic coast. As a result, it was the wild bird that became a major source of food for the settlers—so much so that eating turkey on the first Thanksgiving Day was no treat for the Pilgrims!

Nor did the Pilgrims' relatives in England consider the turkey a treat. By the end of the sixteenth century, turkey had become

31

Turkeys on an experimental farm in Beka, Lebanon

a traditional Christmas dish—although laws had been passed throughout Europe a few years previously "repressing the luxury of serving turkeys." Proof that these laws became obsolete within a short time is furnished by Bartolomeo Scappi, cook to Pope Pius V. In 1570, Scappi published a book of "receipts" for cooking turkey.

Not long after the turkey was introduced into Europe, farmers began selecting breeding stock that would produce larger birds. This was nothing new. Man has constantly tried, for one reason or another, to change the size, conformation, and coloration of all the galliformes that have been domesticated.

Thus, by the time the first Thanksgiving was being celebrated, English poultrymen had developed several varieties of turkeys from their original Mexican stock. Among these breeds were the copper-colored Cambridgeshire, the Suffolk, the White, and the Norfolk. Breeds of turkeys were also being developed elsewhere. For example, in Holland, a buff-yellow bird with a white topknot strutted through barnyards. This bird may be the lineal ancestor of the European White Holland. Actually, there has been so much selective breeding, crossbreeding, and line-

This is a 19th-century artist's impression of the barnyard of a small farm in which the turkey cock seems to be the dominant figure.

A proudly strutting gobbler. Note the snood on the head, the wattle on the neck, and the beard on the chest.

breeding to produce various strains of turkeys that it is extremely difficult to trace the history of some of them.

In common speech, the word turkey is employed to describe both male and female birds. But turkey growers identify the males as toms, gobblers, or cocks, and the females as hens. The technical name for newly hatched birds, irrespective of sex, is poults.

Domestic turkeys of all breeds have certain common physical characteristics. Males are larger than females and have brighter plumage. Toms bear caruncles (prominent fleshy protuberances) on heads and throats. Hens are less carunculated but, like males, have a fleshy process of the skin called a wattle hanging from the throat.

Another fleshlike appendage is located near the base of the bill. When fully developed, this growth, called the snood, becomes quite large, plump, and elastic on males but is small, thin, and inelastic on females. Most commercial breeders remove the snood when their birds are quite young.

When males are about four months old, a tuft of feathers appears on the breast. While this "beard" may be a foot long on a wild cock, those of domestic toms are rarely over six inches. Most females lack the beard and, if present, it is only about an inch in length.

Not only are male's heads coarser and wider than those of females but also the head furnishings are brighter. The tom's head, snood, wattle, and the upper part of the neck are a bright "turkey red." When the bird is excited, the red changes to white overlaid with blue. The deepest shade of blue is in the face. Immature males and all females show only traces of blue coloring.

The plumage of white turkeys often shows specks of black or gray pigment. At times, the feathers are totally or partially off-colored. The eyes of white strains are medium to dark brown; the shanks, feet, and beak are white or pinkish white. No variety of white turkey is an albino. All are "sports," or mutations, in colored breeds, most originating in flocks of Bronze turkeys.

White-feathered turkeys have more plumage than the colored breeds. Because there is a difference in the plumage on the breast of males and females of most colored breeds, poults can be sexed when adult feathers appear at the age of twelve weeks. Not only their distinctive hue and markings distinguish male poults—the little birds begin strutting when only a day old.

Although turkey farmers originally raised the largest birds possible, over the centuries this changed. As families became smaller—and ovens more compact—breeders set out to develop small, broad-breasted turkeys that were economical to raise and ready for market when six or seven months old. Ideally, such

The white-feathered turkeys have more plumage than the colored breeds.

Experiments with wild and domestic turkeys have been conducted to improve breeding stock. Two-year-old brood stock, Missouri.

birds should have legs of medium length, set well apart at the hips, with a plump drumstick, as the lower segment of the leg is called.

A Flock of Turkeys

Certain breeds of turkeys are considered "standard varieties" by the American Poultry Association. Others are not. Nevertheless, two non-standard breeds, the Broad Breasted Bronze and the Broad Breasted Large White, are raised by the millions yearly. These birds and the recognized breeds have the greatest economic value of all varieties of turkeys. Brief descriptions of the turkeys most popular with farmers and consumers follow.

BRONZE. Of all the recognized varieties of turkeys in the United States, the Bronze is the largest. Toms weigh up to fifty pounds,

The Bronze is the most colorful of turkeys.

hens up to fifteen. Originally developed in England, the Bronze, the Broad Breasted Bronze, and crosses between the two are the most commonly raised colored varieties of turkey. The plumage of the Bronze compares favorably with that of its wild ancestor. With white-tipped tail feathers, dull-black wing-feather tips, and bodies sparkling with iridescent reds and greens in front and a bronze tone below, the Bronze is the most colorful of turkeys. Thus it has become the symbol of Thanksgiving.

BROAD BREASTED BRONZE. Like the Bronze, this breed comes from England. Introduced into the United States, it became the most popular breed with turkey farmers. While the Broad Breasted Bronze's coloration is similar to that of the Bronze, the feather tips are apt to be a buffy-white rather than pure white. Moreover, the copper-like bronzing on back, tail, and upper thighs is lacking. Basically it is a black-feathered bird, which gives it dark pinfeathers. The obvious pinfeathers of dark-hued turkeys lower their market value. This is why many farmers raise white-feathered turkeys with inconspicuous pinfeathers.

BROAD BREASTED LARGE WHITE. This breed, developed at Cornell University through selective breeding of Broad Breasted Bronze and White Holland turkeys in the 1950's, has become very popular with turkey farmers. Pinfeathers pose no problem, the breast is broad, and birds can be marketed as heavy roasters when twenty-three to twenty-six weeks old. Meanwhile, twelve-week-old hens can be sold as fryers, while hens twenty weeks old meet the demand for medium-size roasters. At seven months, old toms are marketed as "extra heavy turkeys." This flexibility as to time of sale is an important advantage of the Large White.

BLACK. Known as the Norfolk in England, this breed reveals its ties to *gallopavo* by its lustrous green-black plumage. Undoubtedly developed in Europe from European stock, the Black

A Broad Breasted Large White and a Bronze

is a medium-sized turkey. Males weigh up to thirty-three pounds, females about fourteen.

BOURBON RED. Another medium-sized bird, the Bourbon Red originated in Bourbon County, Kentucky. Few varieties of turkey are more handsome than this bird with its rich, dark, brownish-red body plumage that contrasts with the white wing feathers and the tail. Breeding the Bourbon Red true to color is not an easy task—there is an inherited tendency for the brownish-red hue to fade into a nondescript buff.

WHITE HOLLAND. The White Holland of Europe and the commercially raised White Holland of the United States are two distinct breeds. As indicated, the European variety may have been developed in the Netherlands from a buff-yellow turkey. However, some authorities maintain that the White Holland of Europe was developed from black varieties. There is just as much confusion over the origin of the American bird. Experts

The White Holland House, a restaurant in Broadalbin, New York, once raised the turkeys it serves. These were snapped in the 50's.

41

disagree on whether this medium-sized turkey is a "sport" of wild stock or a Bronze mutation. But, irrespective of its ancestry, the White Holland is a handsome, pure white bird with a black beard, light pinkish-gray beak, and pale pink shanks and toes.

NARRAGANSETT. The early ancestors of this breed were raised in the Narragansett Bay area of Rhode Island, where Norfolks from England were bred with wild turkeys in the 1830's. Eventually, the present strain was established by the Reverend R. H. Avery of New York State who mated a hen from Rhode Island with a huge Bronze cock. Today's Narragansetts have a color pattern very similar to that of the Bronze. In fact, the young poults of both breeds look exactly alike. However, a mature Narragansett's plumage does not have the iridescence of the Bronze.

BELTSVILLE SMALL WHITE. This variety is the result of some twenty years of selective breeding by poultry experts at the United States Department of Agriculture's Research Center in Beltsville, Maryland. The Beltsville Small White was developed to meet the public demand for a small turkey with a broad breast and few pinfeathers, as well as the demand by turkey farmers for a variety that would mature quickly. In order to develop a turkey to meet the needs of both consumer and producer, the Department of Agriculture crossbred half a dozen breeds of domestic turkeys plus wild turkey stock. The resulting small turkey weighs between nine and fifteen pounds and resembles the Broad Breasted White in both color and conformation.

Not only have breeders sought the perfect turkey that would appeal to the general public but also they have developed

The demand for small turkeys increased over many years.

special strains to meet the demand of specialized markets. Other breeds such as the Royal Palm, Nittany, Blue Slate, and Buff Slate are practically ignored by commercial breeders. However, these breeds, along with others having unusual plumage, are raised by hobbyists.

Five

THE TURKEY INDUSTRY

Prior to 1900, turkey raising in America was geared to small-scale production and local sales. Almost all farmers raised turkeys as a secondary crop. An operation was considered to be a large one if it had a thousand birds. Most farms had considerably less.

During the 1920's, large-scale commercial growers emerged, raising turkeys in quantity for shipment to other areas. By the time the United States entered World War II (1941), this type of farming had become a major industry.

Today, the production of turkeys plays a tremendous role in the success of American agriculture. Over ninety million turkeys, second only to chickens among all poultry, are raised each year. Big enterprises dominate the industry. Although independent farms typically average from five hundred to five thousand birds, the largest operations number hundreds of thousands of turkeys.

Minnesota, Iowa, North Carolina, and California are the leading producers, with nearly every state having at least one major

One of the many large turkey farms in Minnesota

operation. Great Britain and Canada also have large numbers of domestic turkeys.

The growth of America's turkey industry is due to a number of factors. Efficient incubators have aided the production of live poults, enabling farmers to raise more adults. Improved breeding and feeding methods have yielded larger birds at a greater profit. Mass-market advertising by the industry as a whole has increased the demand for turkeys throughout the year.

The turkey industry is highly specialized. Some farmers raise breeding stock only—a prize-winning turkey can sell for as much as $4000! Others raise egg layers. A number are engaged in egg

46

A poult is a very young turkey.

production and sell poults. Still others buy poults, which grow into the turkeys that end up on the dinner table. This segment is the largest in the industry.

Styles of turkey raising vary from one part of the country to another. Large operations employ several different methods. On

ABOVE: *Some farmers raise poults.*

LEFT: *Turkeys awaiting their turn at a poultry show. A prize winner can sell for as much as $4000!*

OPPOSITE PAGE: *Some large operations raise turkeys under a roof, the outer perimeter enclosed by wire mesh.*

some big farms, turkeys are raised in compounds that are open to the sky, with tiers of perches, and straw spread out on the ground. In farm "factories," turkeys are crowded into huge buildings. Some operations have groups of pens arranged under a roof, the outer perimeter enclosed by a wall, a fence, or wire mesh. Cages raised several feet above the ground, each containing about a dozen birds, are also common.

Small operations tend to employ barns enclosed on three sides by wire netting with bales of straw on the fourth side. Here, turkeys receive care and attention that is more individualized than on larger farms. Many farmers feel that turkeys do not do well in small pens because of the noise they make and their shy, nervous natures.

ABOVE: *On small farms, turkeys receive individualized attention.*

BELOW: *Turkey growers often group birds by size and weight.*

Some techniques are practiced by all turkey-raisers, regardless of the size of their operation. The birds are grouped according to age and weight. Males are isolated from females except during breeding when the ratio is one tom to every ten hens. If a male is placed in an enclosed area with several females at any other time, he will probably have his tail feathers pecked out! Hens also will peck at the weakest female in a group until she is dead.

The diet of domestic turkeys is totally controlled by man. The turkeys that live in farm factories are given prepackaged formulas prepared by a nutritionist. These birds receive their daily nourishment automatically by machine and are given drugs to increase their egg or meat production. Vitamins eliminate the need for sunlight and exercise.

There is considerable controversy involving this approach to farming. Many people feel that the farm factory environment is cruel and inhumane. Some scientists are concerned about the use of injections containing hormones, flavorings, and phosphates, which are supposed to "improve" the taste and texture of meat. Researchers say that the meat from factory-produced turkeys may actually be lower in protein and vitamins than the flesh of birds reared on natural foods.

A number of small enterprises purchase prepared mixes or use home-grown grain mixed with other feeds to nourish their stock. It takes about one hundred pounds of feed to produce a turkey for market. Old-timers say an occasional treat of fresh violets helps yield tender meat. All operations, large and small, provide a steady supply of clean, cool water.

The weather is probably the greatest concern of all farmers. Turkeys do not do well in damp climates, nor do they respond to extreme heat or cold. In some places, air-conditioners and heaters are employed to control the climate, but most farmers

A load of turkeys ready for shipping to the processing plant

avoid using them due to the added expense of operation.

Production expenses are reflected in the price per pound paid by the consumer. So are transportation and processing costs. Most turkeys are shipped by truck or train to processing plants where they are slaughtered in an efficient and economical manner. Some commercial farmers feel that turkeys are easier to process than other poultry because their feathers are fewer and easily plucked. Of course, there are areas where local turkey growers still butcher their own crop.

Six

A VERY VALUABLE BIRD

When the flesh of a turkey is used for food, it is called turkey. There are two types of cooked turkey—white meat and dark meat.

Although it has an undeserved reputation for being dry, white meat can be moist and juicy when properly cooked. Most white meat comes from the breasts, which yield the greatest amount of protein per pound of all poultry. There is also a substantial amount of white meat on the wings.

Dark meat is located primarily on the thighs and legs. It is famous for its strong flavor, robust tastes, and juiciness.

Most people have a preference for either white or dark meat; some like both. There are many who believe that a taste for turkey must be acquired. Others say it's love at first bite.

Recent studies show that Americans are dining on these bountiful birds in greater numbers than ever before. Over 75 million are eaten each year. This is an increase of about 250 percent since 1950.

It is easy to see why turkey is finding a place on more and

more American tables. If a large number of people are to be fed, it is the least expensive of all poultry—the bigger the bird, the better the buy. About 46 percent of every turkey is edible, which is a higher percentage than chicken or duck. Pound for pound, turkey is usually cheaper than beef, pork, or lamb.

There are many ways to obtain a turkey. At one time, most Americans bought them live from a nearby farmer several weeks before a feast. After bringing it home, the buyer fattened it up in the backyard and butchered it himself. Today, most cities have health ordinances prohibiting this, but the practice is still followed in many rural areas.

The vast majority of all turkeys are purchased from supermarkets and butcher shops. In some places, the entire family can visit a local turkey grower where a suitable tom is selected, slaughtered, plucked, cleaned, and wrapped right before their eyes. While "fresh killed" once applied exclusively to a live bird butchered and sold immediately, this term now refers to any turkey killed from a few days to a few weeks prior to cooking.

Turkeys are generally categorized by size. A small bird weighs from four to ten pounds. A medium bird averages from ten to nineteen pounds. If a turkey weighs twenty pounds or more it is considered to be large.

Age is also used as a description. A turkey under sixteen weeks of age is called a fryer, while a "young" roaster is five to seven months old. A yearling is just over twelve months. Any bird fifteen months or older is considered to be mature.

Since old females generally have tough meat, hens are eaten when they are young and small. Old and large males are usually preferred to young toms because the latter are regarded as having stringy meat.

One way to obtain a holiday turkey is to go to a farm and buy one.

The names given to the different market forms of turkey vary from one part of the country to another. "Whole" or "ready-to-cook" birds have been cleaned and dressed inside and out. A quarter roaster, as the name implies, is one quarter of a turkey. Half roasters are also available. The terms "cut-up," "parts," and "by-the-piece" all refer to specific sections sold separately or by the pound.

In addition to whole birds, halves, quarters, and parts, shoppers will also find a wide selection of commercial preparations. A turkey roast is boneless meat that has been processed, packaged, and frozen. In many cases, artificial preservatives are added to retard spoilage. Turkey roll consists of processed trimmings from the various parts, while turkey breast is sliced meat from the breast of a large bird. Both the former and the latter are popular cold cuts that mix well with ham, cheese, bologna, roast beef, and salami in sandwiches or platters.

Other parts of a turkey are edible, too. Giblets—which include the heart, liver, gizzard, and neck—are generally removed, cooked separately, and used in stew, soup stock, or gravy. The liver is also an ingredient in stuffing.

It would take a larger volume than this to list all the ways of preparing turkey. While roasting is probably the most common method, turkey can also be broiled, barbecued whole on a spit or in parts on a grill, served in a casserole, jellied, curried, fricaseed, or made into chowder and salad.

The author who wrote that ham is "a meat for all eternity" probably never ate leftover turkey. While there are those who dread the thought of having to eat the seemingly endless supply of meat remaining after a turkey dinner, there are others who drool with anticipation every time a platter of these remainders is removed from the refrigerator. True leftover-lovers know that the only barrier to enjoying the distinctive taste of turkey is

Turkey may be served whole or in part. A barbecued turkey breast.

Grilled turkey drumsticks.

LEFT: *Turkey mixes well with other popular meats. Turkey and ham roll-ups are pictured here.* RIGHT: *There are many ways of serving turkey. A wing casserole.* BELOW: *Turkey cutlets and barbecued kabobs.*

A festive whole roast turkey

one's own creativity. Indeed, it would take an eternity to list all the ways of serving unused turkey.

There are still a number of Americans who will only cook a whole turkey on Thanksgiving, Christmas, or a special occasion. Many individuals feel that serving this bird is a solemn tradition reserved for holiday feasts. Others simply do not want to slave over a hot stove for four or five hours more than once or twice each year. For these people, commercial turkey-producers have come to the rescue. Now there are self-basting turkeys and those with a thermometer in the side that pops up when the bird is done.

Turkeys are one of the most widely photographed birds in the United States when cooked. Their images are found in scrapbooks and snapshot albums as well as color-slide and home-movie collections. While some folks say this is due to the custom of photographing all of the food as well as the people at a holiday gathering, others are convinced that it is due to the naturally pleasing sight of a well-dressed, carefully garnished turkey with all the trimmings.

Seven

TURKEY SHOOTING

A turkey shoot and a turkey hunt are two totally different sports. However, they share the same goal—to bring home a bird.

Turkey hunting, which involves first luring a gobbler out of the woods with a bird caller that imitates the sound of a hen and then blasting him with a shotgun, is practiced in every state where there is a substantial wild population. Since free-roaming turkeys are extremely wary, this type of hunting requires a great deal of skill.

As indicated, turkey hunting is strictly regulated. Killing is generally confined to specific months, depending on local conditions. Licenses are issued, with the proceeds going to game management programs and conservation efforts. Quotas (the number of birds that may be killed in a season) are also established. Stiff penalties, including fines and jail sentences, are imposed on both poachers and hunters who exceed their quotas.

In some states, habitats are stocked with wild turkeys to provide hunters with a reliable source of game. Wild turkeys

Today, wild turkey populations are preserved for future generations to enjoy.

native to New Mexico have been imported to Texas in return for birds common to the Lone Star State. In New York and New Jersey, where large-scale abandonment of farmland and its return to forests and woodlands have created habitats for turkeys, there are more and more of the birds.

There are other ways to "shoot" turkeys. In many parts of the country, local organizations such as police and fire departments hold turkey shoots. Most take place during the weeks before Thanksgiving or Christmas. Participants in these contests generally use rifles, shotguns, bows and arrows, or handguns to prove their marksmanship. Actually, no turkeys are shot during these shoots, except possibly paper ones used as targets.

Participating in a turkey shoot is relatively simple. The entrant pays a fee for the opportunity to fire one or more shots at a target that is usually so small or so far away that success is based more on luck than skill. Scoring systems vary according to local custom. Most are based either on points or the number of hits closest to the center of the target. Individuals with the best scores always take home the coveted prize—a turkey for the holiday feast.

Turkey shoots are great fun and excellent ways of raising funds for worthy causes. But there is little chance that they will ever become the national pastime. Similarly, Benjamin Franklin's dream of having the turkey as the symbol of the United States will never come to pass. Nevertheless, these noble birds will continue to be a valuable source of food as well as an important part of American holiday tradition.

Index

Africa, 7, 9
Agriocharis ocellata, 7
American Poultry Association, 37
Art, 20–23
Asia, 11
Audubon, John J., 22
Avery, Rev. R. H., 42
Aztecs, 17, 30

Bacon, Sir Nathaniel, 22
Bassano, Jacopo, 22
Beaumont, Francis, 23
Breeds
   Beltsville Small White, 42
   Black, 41
   Blue Slate, 44
   Bourbon Red, 41
   Broad Breasted Bronze, 37, 39
   Broad Breasted Large White, 37, 39
   Bronze, 37, 39, 43
   Buff Slate, 44
   Cambridgeshire, 33
   European White Holland, 33
   Narragansett, 42
   Nittany, 44
   Norfolk, 33, 39, 41, 42
   Royal Palm, 44
   Suffolk, 33
   White, 33
   White Holland, 39, 41–42
Bruegel, Peter, 21

Central America, 7, 9, 30
Christmas, 32, 59, 62

Cities of Gold, 30
Conquistadors, 20, 30
Cornell University, 39
Coronado, Francisco, 30
Cortez, Hernando, 20, 30

Da Bologna, Giovanni, 23
Dances, 16
De Vlieger, Simon, 21
D' Hondecoeter, Melchior, 22
Dictionary of the English Language, 8

Edward III, King, 9
Elizabeth I, Queen, 23
Elyot, Sir Thomas, 8
England, 9, 30
Espejo, Antonio, 30
Europe, 7

Fernandez, Francisco, 30
Fleming, Marjorie, 23
Fletcher, John, 23
Folklore, 15, 16
France, 36
Franklin, Benjamin, 62
Fuertes, Louis Agassin, 21

Galliformes, 9, 32
Gesner, Konrad, 21
Godey's Lady's Book, 23
Guinea fowl, 7, 8, 9

Hale, Sarah Josepha, 23
Hayes, Rutherford, President, 23
Hazlitt, William, 23

Historia Animalium, 21
Holmes, Oliver Wendell, 23
Hunt, Lynn Bogue, 21
Hunting, 60, 62

Indians, 7, 12, 14, 15, 16, 21
Ireland, 16
Italy, 30

Johnson, Dr. Samuel, 8

Lincoln, Abraham, President, 23, 24
Literature, 23

Medicine, 16
Meleagris gallopavo, 7
Mexico, 12, 20, 30
Montezuma, 20, 30
Mount Tom, 20
Music, 23

Nash, Odgen, 23
New World, 7, 9
North America, 7, 9, 11

Ocellated turkey, 7, 11

Parapavo californicus, 9, 11
Patiank, 16
Peale, Titian, 21
Peterson, Roger Tory, 21
Pheasants, 11
Philippines, 16
Pilgrims, 23, 31
Pius V, Pope, 32
Place names, 19–20
Popular sayings, 18–19

Rancho La Brea, 9
Religion, 12, 14, 15, 17
Rodriguez, Augustin, 30
Roosevelt, Franklin D., President, 24

Scappi, Bartolomeo, 32

Selective breeding, 32
Shakespeare, 23
Smith, Captain John, 19
Spain, 31
Superstitions, 12, 14, 16–17

Thanksgiving, 19, 23–24, 31, 39, 59, 62
The Birds of America, 22
Turkey (domesticated)
  classification, 9–11
  cries, 7
  derivation of name, 7–9
  marketing, 53–54, 56, 59
  physical appearance, 35–37
  raising, 32–33, 45–47, 49, 51, 52
Turkey (wild)
  ancestry, 11
  behavior, 12
  conservation of, 20, 60
  courtship, 26–27
  diet, 25–26
  domestication of, 30, 31
  eggs, 27
  flight, 27, 29
  habitat, 25, 36, 39
  nest, 27
  range, 25, 29
  voice, 29
"Turkey Day," 19
"Turkey in the Straw," 23
Turkey shoots, 62
"Turkey Trot," 16
Turkish Empire, 7

United States, 62
United States Department of Agriculture, 42

Weatherlore, 14, 17–18
Wilbur, Richard, 23
World War II, 45

Yoo, William, 9

64